MONKEYS

alex kuskowski

Consulting Editor, Diane Craig,
M.A./Reading Specialist

Sandcastle

An Imprint of Abdo Publishing
www.abdopublishing.com

visit us at www.abdopublishing.com

Published by Abdo Publishing, a division of ABDO, PO Box 398166, Minneapolis, Minnesota 55439.
Copyright © 2015 by Abdo Consulting Group, Inc. International copyrights reserved in all countries.
No part of this book may be reproduced in any form without written permission from the publisher.
SandCastle™ is a trademark and logo of Abdo Publishing.

Printed in the United States of America, North Mankato, Minnesota
062014
092014

THIS BOOK CONTAINS
RECYCLED MATERIALS

Editor: Liz Salzmann
Content Developer: Nancy Tuminelly
Cover and Interior Design: Anders Hanson, Mighty Media, Inc.
Photo Credits: Shutterstock

Library of Congress Cataloging-in-Publication Data
Kuskowski, Alex., author.
 Monkeys / Alex Kuskowski.
   pages cm. -- (Zoo animals)
 Audience: 004-009.
 ISBN 978-1-62403-273-8
 1. Monkeys--Juvenile literature. I. Title.
 QL737.P9K87 2015
 599.8--dc23

                    2013041834

SandCastle™ Level: Transitional

SandCastle™ books are created by a team of professional educators, reading specialists, and content developers
around five essential components—phonemic awareness, phonics, vocabulary, text comprehension, and fluency—to
assist young readers as they develop reading skills and strategies and increase their general knowledge. All books
are written, reviewed, and leveled for guided reading, early reading intervention, and Accelerated Reader® programs
for use in shared, guided, and independent reading and writing activities to support a balanced approach to literacy
instruction. The SandCastle™ series has four levels that correspond to early literacy development. The levels are
provided to help teachers and parents select appropriate books for young readers.

EMERGING · BEGINNING · **TRANSITIONAL** · FLUENT

CONTENTS

MONKEYS

Monkeys are **primates**.

They live in **tropical** forests.

People see monkeys at the zoo.

AT THE ZOO

Monkeys at the zoo live in a pen.

They have trees and water.

They play with toys.

MONKEY FEATURES

Monkeys use their hands and feet to hold onto branches. Some monkeys use their tails too.

Most monkeys
live in trees. Some
monkeys live on
the ground.

Monkeys live in a troop. They travel together. They look out for each other.

FOOD

In the wild, monkeys eat plants. At zoos, monkeys are given plants and fruit to eat.

BABY MONKEYS

Baby monkeys stay near their mothers. They often ride on their backs.

16

MONKEY FUN

Monkeys **groom** each other.
It helps keep their
fur clean.

Monkeys play and learn together. They **explore** the world around them.

FAST FACTS

- Some people keep monkeys as pets.

- The two main groups of monkeys are Old World monkeys and New World monkeys.

- A monkey was sent into space in 1955.

- Most monkeys have tails.

QUICK QUIZ

1. All monkeys live in trees.
   True or False?

2. Monkeys live alone.
   True or False?

3. Baby monkeys ride on their mothers' tails. *True or False?*

4. Monkeys **groom** each other.
   True or False?

GLOSSARY

explore - move around an area to see what's there.

groom - to clean oneself and take care of one's appearance.

primate - a mammal with developed hands and feet, a large brain, and a short nose, such as a human, ape, or monkey.

tropical - located in the hot, wet areas of Earth.